GW01057492

Original title:
Migratory Mindset

Editor: Jessica Elisabeth Luik
Author: Olivia Orav
ISBN HARDBACK: 978-9916-86-421-0
ISBN PAPERBACK: 978-9916-86-422-7

Ephemeral Daydreams

In the hush of whispered leaves,
Dreams are spun from twilight threads.
Fleeting visions, hearts reprieve,
In the cloud-kissed, starlit beds.

Fantastical reels unwind,
Beyond the clutches of dawn.
Fading, like a fickle mind,
Gossamer, now here, now gone.

In the whimsy of the wind,
Chasing shadows, light as air.
Moments weave, yet still they rescind,
Ephemeral, beyond compare.

Floating realms, both near and far,
Ephemeral daydreams fly.
Catching only what they are,
Echoes stitched upon the sky.

In the dawn, those dreams will part,
And arise with evanescent art.

Invisible Paths

Through the forests thick with green,
Trails unseen, laid soft and clear.
Silent signs in twilight's sheen,
Guiding footsteps, veiled and dear.

Whispered secrets in the breeze,
Mark the way one cannot see.
Boundless maps of hidden keys,
In the hush of mystery.

Questing hearts will surely find,
Pathways laced with ancient lore.
Invisible threads that bind,
Journey's end and something more.

Untouched roads where shadows play,
Lead us to the heart's recess.
In these lands we dare to stray,
Seeking truth in quietness.

Veiled routes that softly blend,
In the invisible paths we wend.

Soulful Sojourns

Through the chambers of the soul,
Journeys carved in silent prayer.
Every step a story told,
Etched in time, eternally there.

Wandering through thoughts profound,
Whispers of the heart's own quest.
Silent echoes all around,
Seeking solace, seeking rest.

In the twilight's gentle glow,
Soulful sojourns find their path.
Into realms where shadows flow,
Calming storms and easing wrath.

Dreams and memories entwine,
On these roads no eyes can trace.
Beyond boundaries of time,
Searching for a sacred place.

Guided by the inner light,
Soulful journeys through the night.

Cognitive Treks

On the peaks of thought we climb,
Scaling heights of pure idea.
Time dissolves, transcends design,
Mind's expanse both vast and clear.

Threads of logic intertwine,
Through the labyrinths we roam.
Mapping realms of the divine,
Every thought a stepping stone.

Synapse fires in silent arcs,
Lighting pathways undisclosed.
Curious minds leave their marks,
In the dark, where insight glows.

Through reflection's deepest maze,
Truths are birthed, and fiction flees.
Every thought a guiding blaze,
In the endless mental seas.

Cognitive treks, bold and free,
Charting vast infinity.

Roving Reveries

Through meadows green, my thoughts do fly,
In twilight's hue, they softly lie.
Whispers of winds in valleys wide,
Echo the dreams that deep inside.

Stars emerge as daylight fades,
Guiding whispers in the glades.
Night's embrace, so calm, so deep,
Cradles roving souls in sleep.

Mountains tall and rivers vast,
In my mind's eye, forever cast.
Journey ends but starts anew,
In roving reveries, dreams come true.

Cosmic Wanderlust

The night sky unfolds its vast embrace,
Stars alight in endless space.
Galaxies spin in cosmic dance,
In wanderlust, my soul is pranced.

Across the void, where comets blaze,
I ride on beams through time's thick haze.
Nebulas whisper secrets old,
In stardust dreams, my heart behold.

Planets twirl in silent grace,
Each with a story, a hidden place.
Among the stars, I find my quest,
Cosmic wanderlust, never rest.

Uncharted Brainwaves

In the mind's uncharted seas,
Thoughts set sail on gentle breeze.
Waves of whimsy, crests of dreams,
Illuminate subconscious streams.

Echoes of ideas yet to form,
Drift in silence, break the norm.
Innovations weave and spin,
In brainwaves' dance, new worlds begin.

Currents strong, they pull, they sway,
Guiding insights every day.
Uncharted paths, so wild and free,
In our minds, infinity.

Nomadic Notions

Windswept dunes and forests deep,
Nomadic notions softly creep.
Paths untrodden call my name,
In whispered tones, they fan the flame.

Cities rise and fade to dust,
In restless hearts, a wanderlust.
Sky and earth, a boundless stage,
Nomadic souls, no cage, no age.

Across the world, in steps untamed,
They leave no trace, yet fate is claimed.
Journey's end, yet stories grow,
In nomadic notions, we let go.

Ephemeral Thoughts

Whispers of dawn, fleeting so light,
Under the moon, cloaked in night.
Moments like leaves, swift to depart,
Silent the echoes inside my heart.

Dreams touch the sky, then disappear,
Waves on the shore, never too near.
Time dances softly, shadows cast,
Holding the now, memories vast.

Glimpse of a smile, gone in a blink,
Words left unsaid, reasons to think.
Transient beauty, petals that fall,
Each second fades, answers the call.

The winds of change, they softly blow,
Turning the pages of stories we know.
In the stillness, the silence speaks,
Ephemeral thoughts, the soul they seek.

Cortex Wanderings

Neurons that spark in twilight hues,
Ideas that flutter, whispers of muse.
Synapses bridging realms unseen,
In the brain's labyrinth, thoughts convene.

Pathways twist, some clear, some grey,
Echoes of dreams in light of day.
Logic dances with abstract art,
In cortex trails, they play their part.

Memories weave, some lost, some found,
Currents of thought in circles bound.
In tangled webs, the mind does roam,
Seeking a haven, finding a home.

Of questions posed and answers sought,
Boundless the lands where minds have fought.
Cortex wanderings, a journey rife,
Charting the mysteries of life.

Restless Reflections

Mirrors of night, shadows that plead,
Restless thoughts, a mind in need.
Quiet whispers in moments still,
Echoes of dreams they strive to fill.

Fleeting visions, like stars they fade,
Whispers of time, serenade.
Reflections ripple, truths unfold,
In the silence, stories told.

Night's embrace, a pensive sigh,
Thoughts that soar, touch the sky.
Memories drift on restless seas,
Anchored hearts and mind's decrees.

Journey within, seek and find,
Captured whispers of the mind.
Restless musings, day and night,
Reflections cast in soft twilight.

Voyaging Mind

Horizons vast, where dreams do sail,
Thoughts like whispers, soft as a veil.
Voyaging far, on seas unknown,
In the mind's eye, we're never alone.

Charting stars in the cosmic night,
Maps of wonder, paths of light.
Questions rise on waves of thought,
In these realms, answers sought.

Voyages deep, some high, some low,
In the rivers of mind, we flow.
Adventures called, the spirit stirred,
In silent realms, where thoughts are heard.

Soul's embark on journeys rare,
In vistas wide, beyond compare.
Voyaging minds with hearts aligned,
In boundless seas, truth we find.

Diaspora of Imagery

Scattered dreams in twilight gleam,
Across horizons wide,
Fleeting whispers, silent screams,
In memories, we bide.

Echoes of a time once known,
Fragments in the air,
Through the realms where thoughts had flown,
In visions, we share.

Shadows dance in moonlit flight,
Patterns in the weave,
Phantoms of a past so bright,
In shadows, we believe.

Wanderers we are by heart,
To distant lands we stray,
In the diaspora, find our part,
In imagery, we stay.

Bound by unseen silken thread,
Stretching far and near,
In the vivid dreams we've led,
Our hearts remain sincere.

Ethereal Expeditions

Beneath the starlit skies we soar,
On wings of midnight blue,
Through realms of myths and ancient lore,
In whispers, we pursue.

Celestial paths our guide entwines,
In cosmic dance, we spin,
Through constellations' sacred lines,
In dreams, we begin.

Eclipsed by the moon's gentle call,
We venture forth anew,
Across the heavens' endless sprawl,
In stardust, we construe.

Beyond the realms of time and space,
In ether's calm embrace,
We journey to that boundless place,
In shadows' soft trace.

Infinite the tales we weave,
In ether's silent glow,
Ethereal realms we shall conceive,
In endless dreams, we go.

Mind's Migration

Through the corridors of thought,
We wander, ever still,
Seeking what the dawn has brought,
In echoes of the will.

Moments drift like autumn leaves,
In winds of time's embrace,
Each a tale that memory weaves,
In the mind's vast space.

Silent pathways, inner quests,
In twilight's tender gleam,
Bearing truths that life attests,
In the gentle stream.

Journeys born of deep desire,
Across the realms unseen,
Guided by an ancient fire,
In colors, rich and keen.

Thus the mind, it roams afar,
In realms both new and old,
Finding solace in each star,
In stories yet untold.

Rambling Ideals

In fields of thought, we freely roam,
Where shadows turn to light,
Casting seeds of dreams we've sown,
In the silent night.

Wandering through the realms of mind,
In whispers soft and clear,
Seeking truths we aim to find,
In ideals, sincere.

Through the haze of crowded streets,
In the clamor, we reflect,
Finding peace where heartbeats meet,
In thoughts, we connect.

Mountains high and valleys deep,
In nature's vast expanse,
Rambling ideals in moments steep,
In life's endless dance.

Ever onward, paths untold,
Our spirits' quest define,
In the search for what we hold,
In dreams, our souls align.

Flights of the Imagination

Across the bounds where dreams take wing,
In endless skies, see visions spring.
A canvas vast, hope's colors blend,
In wonder's realm, where thoughts ascend.

Stars above tell tales untold,
Whispered secrets, brave and bold.
Hearts explore, in silent flight,
On trails carved in the velvet night.

Dawning light in every hue,
Paints the dreams we dare pursue.
From depths uncharted, spirit's call,
Dreams awakened, conquering all.

Cerebral Pilgrimage

Within my mind, a journey stirs,
Paths unseen, with soft murmurs.
Stories ancient, lifetimes past,
Memories' spirit holding fast.

Fields of thought, a pilgrim treads,
With light and shadow, onward heads.
Tracing steps on hallowed ground,
Where knowledge's echo can be found.

Silent halls of wisdom's keep,
Guarding secrets in their deep.
Through each winding turn and gate,
Cerebral roads illuminate.

Wandering Psyche

In realms where quiet musings flow,
The wandering psyche's rhythms grow.
Beyond the grasp of time and space,
To wander free, without a trace.

Ethereal wings of thought unfurl,
Through worlds unseen, they softly swirl.
Emotion's tides, they ebb and flow,
In the psyche's depths, dreams sow.

Gliding through the mind's expanse,
In every whisper, every chance.
Wandering paths of light and shade,
With visions bright, creation's laid.

Mind's Uncharted Travels

Across horizons undefined,
The mind embarks on quests entwined.
Unwritten maps, new paths unspool,
In journeys vast, the spirit's fuel.

Through labyrinthine thoughts, we roam,
In silence, truth becomes our home.
Each step unfolds a hidden scene,
In realms where unknown terrors glean.

A boundless voyage, inner quest,
Navigating dreams abreast.
In the margins of the soul,
Mind's uncharted travels extol.

Nomadic Ruminations

Beneath the endless skies I roam,
Wherever wind and stars do guide,
Thoughts wander as leaves in a storm,
Among the valleys, far and wide.

Each sunset paints a new array,
Of stories woven, told, untold,
In every echo, songs of clay,
The whispers of a heart beheld.

In transient moments, peace I find,
Where mountains kiss the azure seas,
A fleeting touch, the world unwinds,
And sets the seeking spirit free.

Through deserts vast and forests deep,
In shadows dance, by moonlight's gleam,
Footprints fade in sands of sleep,
Yet dreams eternal light my theme.

Infinitesimal Journeys

In realms unseen, the paths arise,
Where atoms weave their subtle grace,
Each step an echo of the skies,
In microscopic, boundless space.

From quarks to stars, the dance unfolds,
In secrets of the cosmic dust,
Infinitesimal tales retold,
With every heartbeat, every gust.

Beneath our gaze, in hidden spheres,
The universe within unfolds,
Each moment, countless light-years near,
As vast dimensions gently hold.

In essence pure, in truth profound,
The endless journeys intertwine,
Through boundless worlds, through silence sound,
In smallest whispers, truths align.

Mental Revolutions

Within the chambers of the mind,
A revolution softly brews,
Ideas and thoughts, in chaos find,
A symphony in colored hues.

The sparks of change ignite the core,
As paradigms in silence shift,
Old walls, foundations, no more floor,
New realms of thinking gently lift.

The chains of stagnant thought released,
Imagination blooms anew,
The quill of wisdom, beauty fleeced,
Crafts futures in a brighter hue.

Through mental strife, through doubt's embrace,
Transformation finds its claim,
A revolution finds its face,
In minds awakened, free from blame.

Spirited Travels of Thought

Through realms of wonder, thoughts cascade,
Beyond the bounds of time and space,
A journey where no maps invade,
The spirit's quest for pure embrace.

In dreams, the wanderer takes flight,
O'er mountains tall, through valleys deep,
In whispers of the silent night,
Where secrets of the cosmos sleep.

Each vision crafts a world anew,
A tapestry of mind's delight,
Where shadows dance and spirits flew,
In dawn's first faded, tender light.

The heart's horizon ever wide,
A boundless sea of hopes and fears,
As thoughts unshackled, free to glide,
In timeless journeys of the years.

Journeys Within

In twilight's hush, where shadows play,
Our spirits roam, a vagrant's stay.
Through dreamscapes vast, unseen, untold,
We chase the echoes of the bold.

Beneath the moon's pale silken light,
We wander far, embracing night.
In whispers soft, the secrets blend,
A labyrinth where we ascend.

Through forests deep, where silence sings,
The heart unfurls its tethered wings.
In mirrored streams, reflections bare,
We find the truths that linger there.

By flicker of the fire's gleam,
We trace the edges of a dream.
In quietude, the soul's refrain,
We seek the self, unearth the pain.

On pathways lit by inner spark,
We journey through the endless dark.
In every breath, a chance to see,
The boundless realms of mystery.

Roaming Reflections

Across the sands, where time does drift,
Our thoughts unfurl, like morning mist.
In every step, a story spun,
Of fleeting days beneath the sun.

With each horizon, wide and vast,
We piece together moments past.
In gazes cast beyond the sea,
We ponder, lost in reverie.

Among the hills, in quiet thought,
We question what the journey brought.
In every shadow, light reveals,
The echoes of our heart's appeals.

Beneath the stars, where dreams reside,
We walk the line 'tween far and wide.
In whispers soft, the past returns,
A silent flame within us burns.

Through meadows green, where flowers bloom,
We find our solace, banish gloom.
In moments still, reflections roam,
We carry forth our inner home.

Ephemeral Cerebrations

In fleeting thoughts, a dance of mind,
We wander realms, both bright and blind.
In whispers soft, our musings flow,
An endless stream of ebb and glow.

Through mazes carved by hand and fate,
We seek the truths that moments state.
In transient dreams, the answers glide,
To questions posed, with time abide.

Among the clouds, where visions curl,
We grasp at wisps within the swirl.
In shadows cast by twilight's brush,
Our musings rise in silent hush.

In whispers caught by evening's veil,
We weave a tale, both bright and frail.
In seconds brief, the mind explores,
The fleeting with, the evermore.

Between the breaths of night and day,
Our cerebrations lead the way.
In moments lost, yet timeless shown,
We traverse thoughts, and stand alone.

Peregrine Thoughtscapes

On wind-swept paths where eagles soar,
Our minds embark, through open door.
In heights unscaled by earthly tether,
We glide through thoughts, like changing weather.

Across the plains of endless skies,
We ponder where the horizon lies.
In each new dawn, a vision born,
Through mental fields, our dreams have sworn.

Through tempest wild and gentle breeze,
Our thoughts traverse with effortless ease.
In whispers of the passing gale,
We write the lines of our own tale.

With wings of wonder, thoughts take flight,
In realms beyond the reach of night.
In each idea, potential spreads,
A landscape where the curious treads.

Beneath the stars' celestial sweep,
Our minds in boundless wonder leap.
Through vistas vast, and valleys deep,
We navigate, in thought, we keep.

Temporal Travels

Through sands of time, we wander true,
In dreams, the past and present brew,
Future whispers softly, new,
Each moment, fresh beginnings accrue.

Footsteps echo on paths unseen,
In realms where shadows softly glean,
Memories and hopes convene,
In the dance of what has been, what'll gleam.

A voyage beyond the ticking clock,
In realms where hands of time unlock,
Secret shores where hours dock,
And eternity holds its silent stock.

Traversing ages, hearts we mend,
Past and present endlessly blend,
In timeless arcs, our journeys send,
Eternal echoes without end.

Beneath the stars, we chart the skies,
In time's embrace, where wisdom lies,
Endless wonders, temporal ties,
We travel on, with open eyes.

Evolving Horizons

Horizons beckon, vast and wild,
Beyond the contours, undefined,
New worlds, like dreams, reconciled,
In ever-changing skyscapes confined.

Mountains rise where seas have slept,
In nature's hands, our futures kept,
Journeys taken, paths adept,
With every dawn, the horizon's swept.

The edge of sight, a canvas broad,
In colors bright, horizons laud,
Paths unknown, by foot they trod,
In steps, the soul's deep effulgence awed.

The morning's breath on fields of green,
As nightfall whispers what has been,
In twilight's hues, horizons glean,
The promise of what's yet unseen.

Through valleys deep and peaks so high,
Our spirits lift to touch the sky,
Boundless dreams where hopes can fly,
Evolving horizons, we live and vie.

Intellectual Exodus

A journey starts in quest of thought,
In realms where ancient minds have sought,
The answers for which hearts have fought,
In wisdom's web, we're dearly caught.

Exploring depths of voiceless night,
In classrooms filled with silent light,
Books and words, our wings for flight,
Ideas born from pure insight.

The mind a traveler, fields of gold,
Where stories, truths, and myths unfold,
Each epiphany, a tale retold,
In mental odysseys, we hold.

Concepts burgeon in fertile lands,
Forged by Nature's unseen hands,
Intellect in cosmic bands,
A universe our thought commands.

Through knowledge realms, our souls transcend,
No limits to the thoughts we send,
In intellectual mounts we wend,
Endless journeys, without end.

Borderless Brainscape

In realms where thought knows no divide,
Ideas flourish, vast and wide,
In intellects, where dreams reside,
In mental waves, our hearts confide.

No borders halt the thinker's quest,
In every mind, the Earth's the best,
Unified, we're truly blessed,
In knowledge shared, our souls invest.

A landscape rich with truths untold,
Thought and wonder, manifold,
In brainscapes where the brave behold,
A future bright and uncontrolled.

In silent thoughts, connections bloom,
Across the world, dissolving gloom,
In ideas' light, we find our room,
United, we'll elude the tomb.

Endless fields where minds commune,
Underneath the same vast moon,
A borderless expanse ensued,
In unity, our lives attuned.

Journeying Psyche

In the depths of silent night,
A spirit roams with gentle might,
Through cobbled paths of ancient town,
Seeking the places wisdom's found.

Veil of stars, a map unrolled,
Stories whispered, truths retold,
Every whisper guides the way,
To a dawn of brighter day.

Mirrors of time, uncharted seas,
Reflecting hopes, reveries,
Through every shadow, fear and fret,
Courage blooms, no regrets.

In the dance of cosmic lore,
Psyche learns what life's here for,
Each step forward, bold and free,
Writes a poem eternally.

Wandering of a Dreamer

Underneath the moon's soft gleam,
Lies the path of wanderer's dream,
Whispers of a future bright,
Painting worlds with silver light.

Echoing through timeless space,
A vision's sweet and tender grace,
Glimpses of a life unknown,
A dreamer's heart, a seed has sown.

Mountains high and valleys deep,
Crystals that in moonlight sleep,
Journey of the soul's delight,
Lost within enchanting night.

Stars that burn and skies that weave,
A mind unchained, a heart believes,
Every step a melody,
Sung in timeless reverie.

Wandering Thoughts

Upon the breeze, thoughts take their flight,
Into the vast expanse of night,
Floating free, without a tie,
Across the endless twilight sky.

Ideas dance on whispered air,
With dreams untold and moments rare,
Through landscapes of both heart and mind,
A treasure trove of truths to find.

Each musing sparks a brightened flame,
Unfurled and wild, they have no name,
Yet every spark, a beacon's light,
Guiding through the still of night.

And as the dawn's first blush appears,
Dispelling all the night's deep fears,
Thoughts descend, serene, at peace,
As morning brings a sweet release.

Transient Souls

Transient souls, like whispers glide,
Through the realms where dreams reside,
Ephemeral as morning dew,
Endless journeys to pursue.

Footprints fade upon the shore,
Trace of lives, forevermore,
Threads of time in silent weave,
Tales of what we give, receive.

In the hush of twilight's glow,
Ancient wisdom starts to grow,
Lessons learned and love that's felt,
Shaping how the heart would melt.

Through the mists, they come and go,
Faces change but spirits show,
Transient yet profoundly whole,
Eternal is the wandering soul.

Whispers of Wandering

Footsteps echo in the twilight glow,
Whispers guide where winds may blow.
Soft murmurs of a distant star,
Leading hearts where dreams are far.

Meadows whisper tales of old,
Secrets in their blooms unfold.
Each petal holds a whispered name,
In the silence, none are the same.

Mountains speak in stony tongue,
Ancient songs forever sung.
Their peaks pierce the sky's expanse,
Through their whispers we take a chance.

Rivers murmur to the shore,
Stories whispered evermore.
In their flow, a path revealed,
Endless journeys unconcealed.

Night whispers to the dawn,
Secrets carried, never gone.
With each new day, a wandering heart,
In whispered dreams, we find our part.

Transient Intuitions

Fleeting thoughts like summer rain,
Hit the soul then go again.
Momentary sparks of light,
Quicken pulse in the still of night.

Ephemeral as autumn breeze,
Lessons learned with casual ease.
Each intuition, brief, concise,
Guiding hearts with silent advice.

Winter frost on windowpane,
Transient truths in icy vein.
Cold clarity that fades so fast,
Yet in moments, shadows cast.

Spring unveils intuitive grace,
Blossoms bloom in a sacred space.
Brief insights in petals pure,
Transient yet they all endure.

Life's wisdom in passing thought,
Transient, never to be caught.
In these moments, clear and bright,
We find our way through transient night.

Veiled Travels

Paths unseen by naked eye,
Hidden roads where shadows lie.
Veiled journeys through the mist,
In the unknown, dreams persist.

Cloaked in mystery's quiet shroud,
Travelers find solace proud.
Through the haze of veiled terrain,
New destinations they attain.

Under moon's elusive glow,
Secret ways the night doth show.
Through veiled travels, souls embark,
Guided by the unseen spark.

Winding trails of fate's design,
Mystic signs in stars align.
Veiled by time, yet ever true,
In these paths, courage grew.

In the veiled, the heart takes flight,
Navigates through dark to light.
Secret journeys undertaken,
In the unknown, fears are shaken.

Mental Trailblazing

Through the mind's celestial maze,
Wandering in a thoughtful haze.
Boundless realms in mental flight,
Trailblazing paths of pure insight.

Each idea a distant star,
Guiding thoughts both near and far.
Mental maps of vast unknowns,
Blazing trails where wisdom's sown.

Psychic forests, dense and deep,
Hidden truths in shadows sleep.
Trailblazing through mental wood,
In such wilderness, finding good.

Mental rivers carve the way,
Ideas flow, thoughts ebb and sway.
Through the currents, we navigate,
Trailblazing minds, no room for hate.

In the landscape of the mind,
Endless paths we seek and find.
Mental trailblazing, ever bold,
In these journeys, hearts take hold.

Sojourner's Insight

Upon the roads less traveled far,
Beneath a sky lit by a star,
A whispering breeze recounts a tale,
Where wanderers thrive and never fail.

Steps unmeasured but deeply felt,
In forest shades where mystics dwelt,
Each footprint marks a quest begun,
A journey of rounds yet to be won.

Mountains speak in tongues of time,
Their echoes ring in silent rhyme,
Valleys hold the dreams we weave,
In the hearts of those who dare believe.

Oceans call with siren's grace,
To horizons' end, endless space,
Where hope and fear entwined will be,
In the vast expanse of destiny.

Lanterns light the darkened way,
With each new dawn, a brighter day,
The sojourner's insight ever clear,
Through shadowed paths, we must adhere.

Meandering Meditations

In quiet fields where silence dwells,
A solitude of nature tells,
Of dreams that float on whispered wings,
And peace that every morning brings.

Through winding streams, our thoughts do flow,
In currents gentle, ever slow,
They weave a tapestry unseen,
Of moments tranquil, pure, serene.

The heart explores, where mind does rest,
In twilight hues, at nature's best,
A canvas vast of greens and gold,
Where stories of the soul unfold.

Beneath the oak, the shadows play,
In gentle breezes, leaves convey,
A symphony of life's refrain,
In meadows bathed by morning rain.

Thus wander we in soft embrace,
Of nature's hand, through time and space,
With meditations meandering free,
In the gentle realm of eternity.

Drifting Cognition

A mind adrift on seas of thought,
In currents deep, reflections caught,
Where shadows dance, and echoes sing,
Of unseen realms and everything.

Through clouds of wonder, dreams ascend,
To heights where earthly bounds do end,
A flight through worlds in star-lit waves,
Where consciousness in silence paves.

In every thought, a galaxy,
Of endless possibilities,
A spark ignites, a story grows,
In the quiet depths where wisdom flows.

Horizons bend in twilight's glow,
Reality, an ebb and flow,
As drifting minds in dreams expand,
Beyond the grasp of mortal hand.

So float we free in cosmic streams,
Through timeless voids and boundless dreams,
In drifting cognition's soft embrace,
We find the keys to inner space.

Restless Muse

A restless muse wanders the night,
In quest of thoughts that soar in flight,
With every star, a tale to tell,
A whispered word, a casting spell.

Through midnight's veil and darkest hour,
It seeks the spark, the hidden power,
In shadows deep, where secrets lie,
Beneath the unobservant eye.

It haunts the dreams of willing minds,
In whispers soft, the lost it finds,
A dance of prose, a melody,
Of unseen wings of poetry.

Each fleeting thought, a seed it sows,
In fertile grounds where passion grows,
To bloom in verses ever bright,
In the dawn of each creator's light.

Eternal muse, forever bound,
In restless search, it circles round,
Unleashing waves of art and grace,
In the endless dance of time and space.

Transient Tranquility

In whispers of the morning dew,
Serenity is born anew.
Fleeting glimpses, calm and bright,
Evaporate with rising light.

Amidst the rustling leaves, a pause,
Tranquil moments, nature's cause.
Elusive peace through branches creeps,
In dawn's embrace, tranquility seeps.

The wind caresses gently still,
Echoes of a distant thrill.
Minutes pass and shadows play,
In transient peace, we find our way.

Underneath the azure sky,
Time's soft touch, a lullaby.
Transient moments forged in gold,
Stories of the quiet told.

Waves of calm by morning cast,
Though the peace may never last.
Ephemeral, yet it leaves a mark,
A fleeting light within the dark.

Vagabond Visions

In dreams unbound by tether's might,
Vagabond visions take their flight.
Through realms unknown and spaces wide,
Where endless possibilities abide.

Wanderlust beneath the stars,
Unseen worlds and distant mars.
Journeys far on paths unseen,
Through waking dreams, where we've been.

Ethereal highways, unseen trails,
Journey through the winds and sails.
Eyes wide open, hearts aglow,
Through the night, we softly flow.

Knapsacks filled with stardust bright,
We traverse in the silent night.
In each step, new visions bloom,
Wandering through the cosmic room.

Nomads of the nebulous night,
Vagabonds in whispered light.
Ephemeral yet deeply clear,
In visions, we are always near.

Ethereal Odyssey

Gossamer threads of twilight spun,
Ethereal odysseys begun.
Through cosmic tides and lunar drifts,
We sail on starlit astral ships.

Mirrors of a distant past,
Reflections in the heavens cast.
Voyages through timeless streams,
In the void, we chase our dreams.

Galaxies in splendor show,
A universe that seems to glow.
Boundless, endless, journeys start,
Ethereal voyages of the heart.

Constellations guide our way,
Through the night and into day.
Voyaging on celestial seas,
Odysseys of mysteries.

Infinite in scope and time,
This odyssey, so truly prime.
In the vast, where stars align,
Ethereal and so divine.

Subconscious Safaris

In the jungle of the mind,
Subconscious safaris to find.
Hidden trails and pathways deep,
Through the wilds, our secrets keep.

Dreams as guides through shadowed trees,
Where thoughts roam and wander free.
At night we travel far and wide,
In the depths where truth resides.

Voyages through veiled terrains,
Mysteries in silence reign.
Memories blend with ancient lore,
Safaris through the inner core.

Lions roaring thoughts aloud,
Beasts of fear in darkened shroud.
Consciousness and dreams entwined,
In safaris, we are defined.

Awakening each dawn anew,
From subconscious realms we flew.
Journeys through the night's expanse,
In dreamland, every thought's a dance.

Serenading Horizons

When daylight's end is gently near,
The sky unveils a twilight tear.
Colors blend in whispered tone,
Serenading dreams unknown.

Hues of amber seize the sight,
While shadows dance in coming night.
Stars emerge in soft array,
To serenade the end of day.

Winds in whispers play their part,
Humming tunes that touch the heart.
Mountains bow to evening's song,
As horizons stretch and long.

Oceans kiss the fading beams,
In the language known to streams.
Serenades to lands afar,
Guided by the evening star.

Wayfarer's Wisdom

Tread the path of dawn anew,
Wisdom's light is gentle hue.
Footsteps echo in the dust,
Time is just and paths are trust.

Mountains call with voices old,
Secrets in their folds uphold.
Wayfarer's heart in wonder beats,
Journey's end and start it greets.

Rivers carve their ancient ways,
Songs of yore and future days.
Wisdom in the water's flow,
Teaches what the soul should know.

In the forest, whispers veer,
Nature's truth is ever near.
Wayfarer, heed the silent call,
Find the wisdom in the thrall.

Journeying Narratives

Pages turn with every stride,
Journeys told, paths not denied.
Tales of wander, legacies,
In the hearts and memories.

Stories etched in every step,
Journeys birthed with every rep.
Legends whispered by the wind,
Journeying where souls are pinned.

Maps of life and paths unknown,
In their quest the seeds are sown.
Narratives of courage, fate,
In each traveler's gait.

Journey long and journey far,
Stories written in the scar.
Every turn and twist a verse,
In the narrative's diverse.

Peripatetic Ponderings

Walking where the mind can roam,
Paths of thought away from home.
Pondering on nature's rhyme,
Steps aligned in rhythm's time.

Trails of wonder, trails of thought,
In each footstep wisdom caught.
Peripatetic heart can find,
In the journey, peace of mind.

Silent musings waltz with breeze,
Introspection under trees.
Ponderings in every hue,
Nature's palette seen anew.

Rambled paths in dusk or dawn,
Ponderings where dreams are drawn.
Peripatetic soul, be free,
In the journey's mystery.

Mental Itineraries

Paths in my mind, winding and clear,
Illusions of places where I hold dear,
Mapping the memories, canvas in hand,
Tracing the stories in invisible sand.

Journeys uncharted, thoughts come and go,
Ripples in time, soft as the snow,
Each destination, a whispering breeze,
Bringing me comfort, putting me at ease.

Dreams intertwine, moments conflate,
Visions of lives in a delicate state,
A mental odyssey, endless and grand,
Guided by shadows cast from distant lands.

Ideas wander, some fast, others slow,
Crafting realities from seeds they sow,
From dawn till dusk, my mind in flight,
Exploring the cosmos through day and night.

No roads to follow, no signs to see,
Endless expanse where my soul roams free,
Mental itineraries, ever so wide,
A universe tethered, deep inside.

Nomadic Notions

Wandering thoughts, unbound and wild,
Silent ponderings of a restless child,
Nomadic notions that twist and turn,
In the labyrinth where hopes do burn.

Arcane whispers call out my name,
In fields of wonder, far from the same,
Drifting on currents of unknown grace,
Seeking the comfort of an unseen place.

Mysteries unfold in secret light,
Glimpses of truths hidden in night,
Where every idea finds its course,
And passion flows like a mighty force.

Questions arise with no clear end,
In realms where fancies and realities blend,
Journeying through worlds not yet known,
Where the seeds of imagination are sown.

These nomadic notions, free and bright,
Guide me through days, and through the night,
Fleeting fancies, each a spark,
Illuminating my mind's dark park.

Mind's Expedition

Embarking on a voyage, within the skull,
Unfurling dreams where truths cull,
Maps drawn from apparitions neat,
Leading me through an abstract street.

Shores unseen and peaks untouched,
Terrains of thoughts so finely clutched,
Stories emerge from silent depths,
Echoes of lives in whispered breaths.

Illusory landscapes, vivid and grand,
Carved by the mind's deliberate hand,
Each turn a revelation divine,
Guiding the soul with a hidden sign.

Through valleys of chaos and peaks serene,
Contrasts in a cognitive scene,
Navigating through questions and thought,
In the labyrinth where wonder is wrought.

Mind's expedition, a constant quest,
Seeking the answers, yearning for rest,
In realms unseen, forever I steer,
Mapping my psyche, year after year.

Drifting Thoughts

Clouds of fancy float on high,
In the vastness of an endless sky,
Drifting thoughts, so gentle and slow,
On cosmic breezes, they come and go.

Unspoken dreams sail without fear,
Through the horizon, ever so near,
Ethereal whispers, fleeting and free,
Traversing an ocean inside me.

Reflections of worlds on sunlight's gleam,
Moments spun from the threads of a dream,
Each reverie a place to dwell,
In the silent corridors where ideas swell.

Ephemeral visions, dancing and light,
Carrying me through day and night,
Their fleeting shadows comfort best,
Offering solace, a place to rest.

With every breath, new paths form,
In a cognitive, perpetual storm,
Drifting thoughts, so soft, so pure,
An eternal journey, forever unsure.

Wanderlust of the Mind

Thoughts meander, mountains climb,
In the valleys back in time.
Whispers of the quiet night,
Feel the pull, the urge to write.

Stars that guide on mental trails,
Tales of oceans, wind-swept sails.
Solitude in crowded days,
In the mind, the wander plays.

Vales of wonder, peaks of dreams,
Rivers, lakes, in thought they gleam.
Boundless realms where spirits soar,
Ever searching, seeking more.

Journeys taken without stride,
Through the landscapes deep inside.
Eyes of wisdom, heart of youth,
Wanderlust to seek out truth.

Silent echoes, distant calls,
Walking through the mental halls.
Maps created, lines erased,
Infinite, the mind's embrace.

Fluid Contemplations

Waves of mind in constant flow,
Ebb and surge, the thoughts bestow.
In the currents, we reside,
Depths of soul, the endless tide.

Ripples form on still, calm seas,
Mirrored skies, soft-swaying trees.
In the silence, whispers speak,
Tales of life, the minds they seek.

Ocean's breath and tranquil gales,
Stories told in moonlit veils.
Dreams dissolve like grains of sand,
In the mind's vast open land.

Moments caught like fleeting spray,
Words unspoken drift away.
Through the channels, far and wide,
Fluid thoughts, a life's high tide.

Liquid grace, the thoughts express,
Sorrows, joys, in pure finesse.
Reflections in the waters bright,
Fluid contemplation's light.

Mental Expeditions

Forms and shadows, inner roads,
Journeys where no path erodes.
Mind, a realm of endless quest,
Seeker of the heart's behest.

Peaks of thought, where spirits soar,
Vistas wide, and evermore.
Mystic valleys, ancient lore,
Mental trails that we explore.

Fields of wonder, plains of dream,
Running rivers, thought's swift stream.
In these lands, we lose our way,
Find ourselves in night and day.

Guided by an unseen hand,
Roaming through this abstract land.
Charting courses, writing lines,
Mental maps, the soul defines.

In the corners of the mind,
Grains of truth, and stillness find.
Expeditions bold and daring,
Paths to which the heart is steering.

Unsettled Reflections

Ghosts of past, in shadows play,
Whispers of a bygone day.
Flickers in the quiet room,
Morning breaks, dispelling gloom.

Fragments of a shattered glass,
Memories through which we pass.
In the heart, the echoes stay,
Words once spoken fade away.

Lingered thoughts and fleeting sighs,
Questions posed in watchful eyes.
Time, it heals, but scars remain,
Unsettled, the silent pain.

Windows to the inner soul,
In the quiet, pay the toll.
Reflections in the dark, profound,
In the silence, solace found.

Endless search for peace of mind,
In the fragments, truth we find.
Equilibrium in plight,
Reflections in the still of night.

Winds of Wandering Thoughts

Across the fields of silent air,
In whispers soft, they gently fare.
Through realms of dreams, they freely spin,
On weightless wings, they flutter in.

They wander past the hills of lore,
Where memories linger, ancient, pure.
With every gust, the past cascades,
In echoes of forgotten shades.

The winds traverse the mind's bright maze,
Unveiling scenes of yesterdays.
They carry hopes, both lost and found,
In secrets whispered, all unbound.

Through valleys deep and canyons wide,
In currents swift, they gently glide.
The murmurs of the winds confide,
In endless journeys, they reside.

So let the wandering thoughts take flight,
Through endless days and starlit night.
For in their breath, alive they keep,
The dreams we've dreamt, the souls we seek.

Mental Nomads

In deserts vast, where thoughts do roam,
The nomad minds find fleeting home.
Across the dunes of shifting sands,
They navigate with knowing hands.

Their paths entwined in transient ways,
Through nights that blur and endless days.
They seek the skies in starlit swirls,
Among the cosmos, dreams unfurl.

These wanderers, with open eyes,
Survey the realms of hidden skies.
Within the void, they chart their course,
In silent whispers, find their force.

Through mental plains, they stride alone,
On quests for truth to call their own.
No roots bind down their seeking selves,
They delve as deep as time itself.

Oh, mental nomads, forever free,
In boundless thought and endless sea.
May journeys lead where none have trod,
In search of wisdom, truth, and God.

Journeys Through the Subconscious

Beneath the conscious veil, we tread,
Into the realms of swirling dread.
Through paths unseen by waking eyes,
In silent whispers, truth belies.

We sail on nightmares, fleeting swift,
In shadows deep, the curtains lift.
The mind reveals what day conceals,
In hidden thoughts, the soul appeals.

In labyrinths of past and fear,
We wander through our psyche's sphere.
Each step unfolds a buried sight,
In pockets of the tranquil night.

Through dreams, we travel worlds unknown,
Into the depths as seeds are sown.
The subconscious holds keys unseen,
Unlocking truths in realms serene.

So let us tread these mystic ways,
Beyond the sun's bright, blinding rays.
In darkened depths, we'll find the gleam,
Of answers whispered in our dreams.

Transitory Dreams

In fleeting moments, dreams arise,
Like morning mist 'neath sunlit skies.
They shimmer bright, then fade away,
Eluding grasp at break of day.

These dreams, ephemeral and kind,
Emerge from depths of slumbered mind.
With light they dance, with shadows play,
Then softly, gently drift away.

In twilight's grasp, where dreams take flight,
They paint the canvas of the night.
With colors drawn from heart's deep well,
In transient tales, they rise and swell.

While time flows on its endless stream,
These visions touch, then leave unseen.
Yet in their wake, they softly leave,
A trace of hope that minds conceive.

Through transitory dreams we wade,
In mystic realms where thoughts cascade.
Within their fleeting grace, we find,
A glimpse of the eternal mind.

Mapless Mindscapes

In realms where no maps chart our way,
We wander wild, both night and day.
Thoughts drift like clouds in sky so wide,
In mapless mindscapes, we confide.

Dreams unfurled in boundless air,
Hopes and fears entwine with care.
Uncharted paths we dare to tread,
In mind's vast seas, both born and bred.

Visions of future, echoes of past,
Moments fleeting, forever cast.
No compass guides, yet forward we stride,
In mapless lands where truths reside.

Through deserts dry and forests dense,
Emotions raw, intense, immense.
Journey on, the heart's desire,
Through mental scapes, we never tire.

In shadows deep and mornings bright,
We lose our way, yet gain new sight.
For in the unknown, we find our grace,
In mapless mindscapes, endless space.

Inconstant Whispers

A whisper passed on autumn's breeze,
Soft voices dance among the trees.
Unseen murmurs, secrets caught,
Inconstant whispers, unseen thought.

Through the night, a gentle sigh,
Words unspoken, drifting by.
Fleeting phrases, hardly heard,
Inconstant whispers, like a bird.

From lips to ears, an echo's trail,
Stories woven, frail and pale.
Each word a ghost, a fleeting breeze,
Inconstant whispers, without cease.

Minds converse in silent tone,
Unseen tendrils, softly grown.
Messages in shadows' fold,
Inconstant whispers, tales untold.

By dawn's light, they fade away,
Yet in our hearts, they always stay.
Transient voices, lost in time,
Inconstant whispers, endless rhyme.

Pilgrimage of Thought

Through winding lanes of mind we go,
A pilgrimage where ideas flow.
Each step a question, each turn a clue,
In thought's vast realms, the old and new.

Wisdom's beacon lights our trek,
Through valleys deep and mountain's neck.
In labyrinths of reason's might,
We seek the truth from dark to light.

Paths converge, then diverge wide,
In silent realms where thoughts reside.
Contemplation's sacred quest,
On journeys long, we find what's best.

With every stride, our spirits rise,
Exploring all that's wise and wise.
In pilgrims' hearts, the fire's bright,
A soul's pursuit of endless sight.

From dawn till dusk, we wander far,
Guided by a mental star.
In quest for knowledge, we are caught,
This pilgrimage of endless thought.

Fluid Fancies

In streams of dream where fancies flow,
Imagination's rivers go.
Unbounded by the shores of real,
In fluid fancies, truths conceal.

Waves of wonder, currents swift,
Ideas rise and set adrift.
Through waters deep and clear as glass,
In fluid fancies, moments pass.

From thought to vision, seamless blend,
In ever-changing streams that bend.
Color, light, and shadows dance,
In fluid fancies, hearts enhance.

A ripple here, a whirlpool there,
In minds so free, beyond compare.
Creation's flow in endless trance,
In fluid fancies, life's advance.

Beyond the realm of black and white,
We drift in hues, both dark and light.
In liquid dreams, we find our way,
In fluid fancies, night and day.

Journeying Psyche

Through realms of thought and dream we sail,
With minds uncharted, hearts unveil,
Into the depths where shadows play,
In silent whispers, night to day.

A lantern glows in twilight's breath,
Guiding souls through life and death,
In mirrored pools, reflections gleam,
Behold the waking of a dream.

From stardust trails to cosmic binds,
We forge ahead with willing minds,
And in the dance of endless skies,
Our spirits rise, our vision flies.

The labyrinth within us swirls,
A tapestry of tangled worlds,
Yet in each thread there lies intent,
A map to which our fate is bent.

Oh journey vast, oh voyage deep,
In waking hours and drifting sleep,
May each step find its destined mark,
A beacon bright within the dark.

Pilgrim of Ideas

A wanderer of thoughts am I,
Across the seas where notions fly,
Through fields of wisdom, mountains tall,
I seek the truths that shape us all.

The compass spins, the winds exhort,
On pathways old where sages sort,
In caverned halls of ancient rhyme,
I trace the echoes lost to time.

Among the clouds of doubt and grace,
I find the light in every place,
In every stone, in every leaf,
An emblem deep of joy or grief.

The roads converge in twilight's hue,
A merging of the old and new,
And onward still my spirit wends,
Where knowledge starts, and never ends.

For I, a pilgrim, ever rove,
In search of wisdom's boundless trove,
May every thought and dream unite,
To cast an everlasting light.

Fleeting Contemplations

In moments brief, the mind will stray,
To realms unknown, so far away,
Where fleeting thoughts like petals blow,
And wisps of dreams begin to grow.

A thousand tales in silence writ,
Emerge from shadows bit by bit,
As whispers soft in twilight's ear,
Unfold the secrets we revere.

The dance of time, a waltz so light,
Enfolds the day into the night,
And through the veils of doubt and fear,
A spark of clarity draws near.

In mirrors dark, reflections gleam,
Of hopes and fears in every dream,
A fleeting glance, a passing sigh,
As endless questions wing and fly.

Oh transient thoughts, oh moments rare,
That weave a story, pure and fair,
In brief sojourns of mind and heart,
A tapestry of life to chart.

Transient Reveries

In quiet hours when dusk descends,
The mind to gentle fancies bends,
Through vistas wide and valleys deep,
We wander realms while thoughts do sleep.

A fleeting brush with worlds unseen,
In twilight hues of golden sheen,
Where every whisper, every sigh,
Becomes a note in night's soft cry.

As stars unveil their ancient light,
We drift on dreams, serene in flight,
In transient reveries we find,
A solace for the restless mind.

The moon, a guardian pale and bright,
Guides us through the velvet night,
In soft embrace of shadows' call,
We find a place where worries fall.

Oh gentle dreams, so briefly here,
Enchant our hearts, dispel our fear,
May every reverie, though swift,
Bestow upon our souls its gift.

Nomadic Echoes

In deserts vast, where winds do shout,
Whispers of the past, they cast about.
Nomadic souls in twilight's glow,
Through time, their echoes softly flow.

Steps on sands by moonlight's gleam,
Life's transient dance, a fleeting dream.
Stars confide in secret lore,
Ancient truths we can't ignore.

Shadows blend with sunlit rays,
Fading paths in endless days.
Through valleys deep and mountains high,
Nomadic echoes never die.

Silence hums its gentle tune,
Underneath a silver moon.
Ancient echoes intertwine,
In every heart, a hidden sign.

Boundless tides and shifting lands,
Time slips through our open hands.
Nomadic whispers, soft and low,
In timeless dreams, forever flow.

Vagabond Dreams

In starlit nights, where dreams take flight,
A vagabond's heart seeks the light.
Roaming lands where wild winds dance,
Wandering souls in lost romance.

Through forest depths and ocean's call,
With hope as guide, they shun the thrall.
Twilight whispers secrets old,
In vagabond dreams, stories told.

By rivers' edge and mountain peak,
In whispered tones, the spirits speak.
In every breeze, a tale unfolds,
Of wanderers brave and hearts of gold.

The open road, a siren's song,
Where restless spirits float along.
In dreams, they find their fleeting grace,
In every new and wondrous place.

Endless horizons, skies of blue,
Through vagabond dreams, skies so true.
With every step, new paths they weave,
In restless hearts, they still believe.

Ephemeral Journeys

Through veils of mist, the dawn appears,
Ephemeral journeys free of fears.
Moments fleeting, like morning dew,
In ethereal hues, the world anew.

In whispers soft, the heart aligns,
With journeys brief, through space and time.
Every step a transient grace,
In fleeting glimpses, we find our place.

Fields of gold where breezes play,
In ephemeral light of break of day.
Journey onward, with eyes aglow,
Through ephemeral paths, our spirits flow.

A tapestry of moments spun,
Underneath the warming sun.
Ephemeral as the lunar tide,
We journey through life, side by side.

In twilight's kiss, the journey ends,
Our pathways blend, like lifelong friends.
Ephemeral as the stars above,
Each journey marks our endless love.

Roaming Reflections

In mirrored lakes, where dreams are born,
Roaming reflections, hearts forlorn.
Journeying far on paths untold,
In wandering thoughts, the soul unfolds.

Through forests deep and cities bright,
Reflections dance in morning light.
Every shadow, every gleam,
A roaming heart in silent dream.

Beneath the skies in twilight hue,
Roaming minds seek truths anew.
Each reflection, a story told,
Of wandering spirits, brave and bold.

In desert winds, through canyons wide,
Roaming thoughts like rivers glide.
Infinite as the boundless sea,
Reflections roam eternally.

Unity in solitude, found,
Roaming hearts in world unbound.
Reflected in life's endless streams,
Roaming thoughts and timeless dreams.

Unravelling Landscapes

Under skies where mountains creep,
Silent whispers from valleys deep,
Rivers carve their endless trail,
Nature's breath, a calming gale.

Forests dark, a realm of green,
Mossy paths, a hidden sheen,
Whispers of the ancient trees,
Echoes carried on the breeze.

Golden fields where sunsets lie,
Rolling hills 'neath twilight sky,
Earth and heavens softly blend,
Horizons that seem without end.

Canyons carved by hands of time,
Secrets locked within their rhyme,
Every grain and every stone,
Stories etched, yet rarely known.

Deserts vast where shadows play,
Sand dunes shift in soft ballet,
Moonlit nights with stars so bright,
Guiding souls by silver light.

Psychic Travels

Through a dreamscape, mind unfurls,
Mysteries in cosmic swirls,
Astral planes and silver streams,
Carrying thoughts and hidden dreams.

Ether's touch, a soft caress,
Guides us through each boundless guess,
Journeys through the realms unseen,
Where reality meets between.

Stars align in cryptic lore,
Galaxies we can't ignore,
Whispers from a distant shore,
Expand the soul, forevermore.

Crystalline visions, clear and bright,
Illuminate the endless night,
Farthest corners of the mind,
Wonders no longer confined.

Onward, upward, floating free,
Embracing every mystery,
Psychic travels, boundless flight,
In the depths of endless night.

Tranquil Journeys

Gentle paths through gardens green,
Ponds where lilies float serene,
Whispers of the fragrant air,
Bid farewell to every care.

Meadows bathed in morning light,
Dew-kissed petals shining bright,
Footsteps soft upon the trail,
Wandering through each quiet vale.

Serenade of autumn leaves,
Rustling in the calming breeze,
Woodland songs and babbling streams,
Guide us through our peaceful dreams.

Clouds drift slowly in the blue,
Framing skies of every hue,
Serenity in every breath,
Walking paths where silence saith.

As the day gives way to dusk,
Shadows deepen, colors flush,
Nature's lull, a gentle plea,
Embrace the tranquil, wild, and free.

Ephemeral Passages

Moments fleeting, like a sigh,
Echo through the evening sky,
Time slips through with whispered grace,
Lingering in the shadowed space.

Petals fall from blooms once bright,
Dancing in the soft moonlight,
Life unfolds in transient ways,
Fading with the end of days.

Waves that kiss the sandy shore,
Retreating to return once more,
Ephemeral as the sea,
Caught between the was and be.

Stars that glimmer, twinkling high,
Disappear from morning sky,
Time withholds no lasting claim,
Burning brief in cosmic flame.

In each passage we shall find,
Ephemeral, by fate designed,
Cherished whispers, fleeting glow,
Love that blooms, then bids adieu.

Shifting Realities

In dreams, the worlds do twist and splay,
Colors melt in bright array,
Truths, like shadows, blend and fray,
Where night dissolves the light of day.

Mountains rise to kiss the sky,
Rivers whisper, running high,
Stars align, like fate's own tie,
In this realm, no rules apply.

Time bends gently, soft and slow,
Moments whisper, ebb and flow,
New horizons dare to glow,
In these realms, we're free to go.

Silent echoes start to sing,
Wings unfold from hidden spring,
Every challenge holds a ring,
In the shifting realms of everything.

Awake, we find we're born anew,
With dreams that paint our skies in blue,
In shifting realms, we see what's true,
Reality's dance is our debut.

Restless Reflections

Beneath the moon's soft, silver gaze,
Recollections blur in haze,
Restless thoughts in endless maze,
Searching through life's fleeting days.

Mirrors show a face unknown,
Souls reflect in undertone,
Echoes from the past have grown,
Haunting fears we had outgrown.

Waves of doubt wash on the shore,
Questions haunt us evermore,
Answers drift, a distant lore,
Restless minds in search explore.

Silent whispers, long suppressed,
Yearnings leave the heart distressed,
Seeking peace, the soul shall quest,
Through the night, we shall not rest.

As dawn breaks, the world anew,
Reflections still our thoughts construe,
Restless minds seek clearer view,
In the morning's gentle dew.

Vagrant Visions

In the alleys of the mind,
Visions vagrant, hopes combined,
Wandering paths so undefined,
Dreams and truths are intertwined.

Ghostly figures cross the lane,
Mirage dancers, bold and plain,
Reality becomes arcane,
In this world, we break the chain.

Every shadow hides a tale,
In the whispers of the pale,
Justice wavers, truths unveil,
Dreamers' ships will set their sail.

Voices from the distant past,
In this moment, shadows cast,
Future's echo, auspic's mast,
Through these visions, we're steadfast.

In the mist, the sight is clear,
Vagrant visions persevere,
Past and future drawing near,
Dreams as guides, we find our gear.

Adventurous Aegis

Beneath the stars, with hearts so bold,
Seek the stories yet untold,
Through the wild, our tales unfold,
With an aegis made of gold.

Forests whisper ancient lore,
Mountains guard their secrets store,
Rivers guide us to the core,
As we venture evermore.

Courage holds the light we seek,
Bravery's what makes us unique,
Fears will falter, shadows bleak,
Adventurers, the strong, the meek.

Hearts as shields, with wills of steel,
Every journey's wound we heal,
Each new quest strengthens zeal,
Through the trials, we reveal.

At journey's end, with tales to share,
Every scar a badge we wear,
Adventurous aegis, beyond compare,
In life's grand venture, we declare.

Odyssey of the Mind

In the realm where thoughts collide,
Dreams and ideas open wide.
Whispers of wisdom start the tide,
An odyssey where none can hide.

Navigating through fields of thought,
Clarity and confusion brought.
In the midst of battles fought,
Victory in each insight caught.

With imagination as the guide,
Thoughts in endless currents ride.
From doubt, we cannot always hide,
Yet hope and truth walk side by side.

Hidden gems within the mind,
Treasures in each layer find.
The quest, though often unrefined,
Leads to depths where souls have dined.

As we journey, hearts align,
Wonders through the dark entwine.
In this voyage, pure and fine,
Odyssey of the mind divine.

Voyaging Notions

Sailing through seas of thought,
Ideas in each wave caught.
Currents to new worlds brought,
Inspiration never distraught.

Tales of lore in every breeze,
Mysteries unfold with ease.
Whispered secrets from the trees,
Harvested as moments seize.

Stars above as guides do gleam,
Lighting paths within our dream.
Boundaries blur, the world a theme,
Nothing ever as it seems.

Through the tempest and the calm,
Ideas soothe like healing balm.
In the chaos, there's a psalm,
Guiding minds with gentle palm.

Voyaging notions never rest,
Questing minds forever blessed.
In pursuit, we find our best,
Thoughts and dreams put to the test.

Wanderer's Whimsy

With every step, the world unfolds,
A tapestry of tales retold.
Journeying through lands of gold,
Mysteries and wonders bold.

The path unknown, a sacred quest,
Adventure in each breath expressed.
In every whim, the heart is dressed,
With curiosity never repressed.

Mountains high and valleys deep,
Secrets within the forest keep.
In shadows where the whispers sleep,
Dreams and visions softly creep.

Meadows where the blossoms bloom,
Pockets of tranquility loom.
In every corner, space for room,
To let the wandering thoughts consume.

In this journey, pure delight,
Stars that guide through darkest night.
In every whisper, every sight,
Wanderer's whimsy takes its flight.

Perpetual Quest

In the heart and in the soul,
Lies a journey to make us whole.
Endless paths to reach the goal,
Seeking truths to make us bold.

Through deserts vast and oceans wide,
The questing spirit cannot hide.
With every step and every stride,
In the journey, we confide.

Questions echo through the night,
Guiding stars that shine so bright.
Search for meaning in the light,
In clarity and in the fright.

Every trial and every test,
Marks the journey, none the less.
In the struggle, we invest,
In the dream of betterness.

The perpetual quest remains,
Through joy and through the pains.
In our hearts and in our brains,
The search for truth forever reigns.

Passing Meditations

In the twilight's tender hue,
Thoughts like whispers softly grew.
Dreams that frolic in the breeze,
Carve their tales on moonlit seas.

Starlit nights and shadows blur,
Silent echoes softly stir.
Minds adrift on waves of time,
Singing wordless, haunting rhymes.

Leaves that shiver in the light,
Canvas painted by the night.
Contours shift and patterns weave,
Secrets that the dusk conceive.

Whispers floating on the air,
Ephemeral, light as prayer.
Time's caress both fierce and kind,
Gentle on the seeker's mind.

Questions linger, answers fade,
In this quiet, starlit glade.
Journey inward, sight unseen,
In the calm, where thoughts convene.

Fugacious Fantasies

Fragments of a fleeting dream,
Flow like murmurs through a stream.
In the dance of twilight's beam,
Hope and wonder softly scheme.

Butterflies of thought descend,
On the winds of dreams they blend.
Colors burst and skies extend,
Time and space both start to bend.

Stars are woven into night,
Truth and fiction intertwine.
Every shadow finds its light,
In the realm of the divine.

Beneath the moon's enchanting glow,
All the tales of time bestow.
Every fantasy we sow,
Blossoms in the twilight's flow.

Transient dreams and fleeting sigh,
Wings of whispers softly fly.
In the heart where fancies lie,
Infinite, the starry sky.

Nomadic Whispers

Echoes in the silent night,
Drifting whispers take to flight.
Stories told in shadows' ease,
Of the ancient, wandering breeze.

Paths that cross where mavens tread,
Songs of old that gently spread.
Nomads' tales of distant lands,
Scribed in time by unseen hands.

Stars their faithful eyes behold,
Mysteries of stories told.
Ancient voices softly sing,
To the night's calm, tender cling.

Footsteps light on virgin sand,
Wisdom carried, gently fanned.
From the dusk till breaking dawn,
Legends of the ever-gone.

Whispers travel, never cease,
In the night, they find release.
Journeys etched in starlit lore,
Nomads' tales forevermore.

Mental Voyage

Voyage through the mind's expanse,
On the wings of thought's advance.
Oceans vast of inner space,
Mysteries that thoughts embrace.

Sailing through the dreams unseen,
Journeys to what might have been.
With every turn and twist of fate,
New horizons contemplate.

Clouds of doubt and waves of hope,
Endless seas on which we grope.
Navigating light and dark,
Guided by the inner spark.

Horizons shift in mental sea,
Dreams and reality agree.
Lands of wonder, sights immense,
Traverse the void, the heart's defense.

Voyage long in silent thought,
Treasures of the soul are sought.
In the mind's vast, boundless sea,
Find the truth that sets us free.

Roaming Reverie

Through fields of gold where shadows play,
Lost in dreams at end of day,
Whispers of wind in silent rhyme,
Echoes of a forgotten time.

With every star, a gentle sigh,
Painting stories in the sky,
The moonlight's touch, a soft caress,
In night's embrace, I find solace.

Mountains tall and rivers deep,
In this world of waking sleep,
A journey far through night and gleam,
A wandering soul in twilight's beam.

Beneath the trees where secrets hide,
Nature's whispers on every side,
In the stillness, hearts can hear,
The silent song that draws us near.

Eyes closed to the world we know,
Into the unknown we dare to go,
In roaming reveries, we find,
The boundless realms within the mind.

Mental Escapades

In corners of a restless mind,
Thoughts that twist and intertwine,
Dreams unfurl with wild delight,
Chasing shadows through the night.

Labyrinths of abstract thought,
Every twist and turn is sought,
Through mazes deep, perceptions change,
On mental escapades, thoughts arrange.

Ideas bloom like springtime's breath,
Awakening from the sleep of death,
In this garden, wild and free,
A mind explores its destiny.

Whispers of the unseen realms,
Guiding hands at mental helms,
Across vast seas of unseen grace,
An endless quest, an endless chase.

In these escapades, the heart can find,
Hidden truths within the mind,
A journey not of step, but thought,
In every dream, a reality brought.

Voyaging Visions

Across the seas of waking dreams,
Where nothing's ever as it seems,
The soul embarks on voyages grand,
Seeking lands of fate unplanned.

Waves of time and tides of fate,
Drawn to shores both love and hate,
Each vision conjured from the deep,
A memory that the heart will keep.

Skies of violet, oceans wide,
In every tide, the world's implied,
Journeys hauled by star and wind,
In voyaging visions, truths rescind.

Each horizon, a whisper soft,
Guiding ships aloft, aloft,
Through storms of doubt and calm collective,
In visions' voyage, we're reflective.

Paths unknown and quests untried,
With every sight, a truth implied,
In voyaging visions, the heart discerns,
The lessons life so subtly learns.

Temporal Wanderings

Through avenues of time we wend,
Past and future gently blend,
Moments stitched in a vast array,
Temporal wanderings day by day.

Whispers of forgotten years,
Echoed laughter, silent tears,
Through the corridor of age,
Life's story written page by page.

In every shadow, light prevails,
Through the winding, timeless trails,
Seek the wisdom lost in time,
In every heartbeat, life's own rhyme.

Memories like autumn leaves,
Carried by the gentle breeze,
Scattered in a dance so free,
Temporal wanderings, just you and me.

Every second, a fleeting glance,
In time's embrace, a sacred dance,
Through temporal shifts, our souls do find,
The endless journey of humankind.